DREAMER

Shane Alan Frederick

Copyright 2008 Laura Frederick
ISBN 978-0-6151-7988-9

Shane's Story

"No one really knows
what's waiting in their future,
where they will be,
who they will be with.
No matter how we look at it,
life will happen,
and when it has passed
we've either made the most of it or we
haven't."

This is a quote from our son, Shane's, college entrance essay, that epitomizes how he lived his life…to the limit. He believed in living life to the fullest.

From the time Shane was about 4 years old he loved wrestling. Many evenings were spent diving off the arm of the couch onto either his Ultimate Warrior doll or his dad, Craig. He and his sister Amanda never tired of play talking their wrestler and superhero dolls. Their commentary kept us entertained for hours. He went on to wrestle in Middle and High School and was looking forward to wrestling in college. J Robinson's Intensive Wrestling Camp was his idea of fun in the summer. He was known for his determination and spirit.

Traveling was a favorite of our family and by the time Shane was in high school he had traveled all over the US as well as Austria, Mexico, Jamaica, Australia, France and Holland. I am certain one of the highlights was his wrestling trip to China. Our last trip together to Paris and Amsterdam for Shane's high school graduation will never be erased from our memories. His next destination was to be New Zealand.

Writing was an integral part of Shane's life early on. He wrote fantasies, lyrics, poetry, elaborated his views on political issues, and documented happenings and highlights of his life. Friends were often a topic or an audience for his writing:

Today was a splendid day,
you see my friends,
I traveled far off and away
from the common chaos that we face.
For in my mind I was in outer space.
Riding on the back of a wild lion…
holding it down for Zion.
Today was unlike the rest,
I was out of my mind I must confess,
and (if) I may seem to be unfair…
You too can lose your mind
and meet me there!

Our family attended the Lutheran church and Shane had strong Christian beliefs. He was never afraid of death, but looked at it as another level of life. He even planned whom he'd like to talk to in his afterlife, naming his 3 uncles, as well as Bob Marley and Jimmy Hendrix.

Didn't see my life pass
Slipped out of my hands
Didn't see the transaction
From the boy to the man,
Now I am company
At my family's Christmas feast
As peaceful as the ocean's tide
As scary as hell's beast
Feel blessed to have
The loving family I do
One that will have a plate
At the table always waiting for you.

After a career fair in eighth grade, Shane became focused on his goal to go into nursing. He was an incredibly caring individual. He took classes all through high school and became a Certified Nursing Assistant when he graduated from Page High School. During Shane's senior year, he began to think about college with the two goals of nursing and wrestling. His experience with the coach from Buena Vista at J Robinson and his interest in attending Dubuque University, also in Iowa, led to our trip in the spring to meet with potential coaches and talk to advisors about the best plan for Shane. He chose Dubuque and we moved him to campus in August of 2006.

Life is full of decision making. We will never know what made Shane decide to go to the party after the Dubuque/ Loris game. We also will never understand why he went out onto the roof when the police showed up. We do know that Shane was a rock climber and was not afraid of heights, but alcohol impaired his common sense and ability to stay on the roof that night, and he fell. In that split instant our bright star was taken from this world. All our hopes and dreams of the future for our son were suddenly irrevocably changed. Because of that lapse in judgment we (and his friends and family) will have to learn to go on without Shane. We are confident we will see him again, but meantime, our hearts are broken.

>   Looking up to the stars,
>   What's out there for me?
>   Wouldn't accept nothing less but
>   A world full of dreams.

Shane Frederick   1987-2006

Friends and Family

Life

Live your life however you want to,
Don't fall to the level of those who taunted you,
Life can be taken away at any minute,
If you mistreat It and offend it,
See friends die and it's already too late,
Time is up, there's no rescheduling for a later date,
Lying in the grave you realize life just passed by,
Too late now at the point of no return,
Can't change decisions it's too late to learn,
Life can be taken away at any minute,
It's not your choice, God will end it

Friends

Throughout all these sins,
be thankful you've got friends,
when your love turns into hate,
it is already too late,
to take back what you've done,
when the end of this world has begun.

You find yourself all alone,
maybe if you used a different tone,
you'd have a true companion beside you,
one that loves you enough to help you get through.

Friends and family is all I got,
I chose to love while others fought,
even with the enemies,
I used love and passion as my only remedies,
throughout my bad decisions,
and all the brutal collisions,
I just hope in the end I'll still have a friend.

Forever Brothers

We've been friends for so long
No matter how many fights we've been in
If you think I'll turn my back you're wrong
No matter what sin you live in
I'll be by your side that's a given
Don't think twice about my loyalty
You feel down and alone
Come take a stroll with me
Just want you to remember you always got a
    brother
Who will be by your side
One who will tell you he loves you when
    you're too @#%$#&' fried
One who will be there through thick and thin
A friend that will be there no matter what shit
    you get in
Make a promise to me that you feel the same
    way
Can I call you my brother any given day?
Make a promise to me that when I die,
You won't forget about me and don't even cry

Friends = Family

My friends are my family, they'll always be there
My friends are my family
We run these streets without fear, without feelings
We run and hide from the hogs evil doings
My friends are my family they're by my side
No need to be scared
My friends are my family even those who have died
They left me one gloomy night
Return to watch over me a black fills the sky
And leave once again with a tear in your eye
My friends are my family they are one in the same
They'll always be waiting, if I go Insane.....

A Little Bit Of Reason

A little bit of reason
A little taste of rhyme
Find myself some lyrics
Buy myself some time

Put two and two together,
Find what I'm looking for
Keep the rhythm going
With a trip to the liquor store

Find myself a reason
Look what I'm fighting for
Hard to make the music
With police at the door

A little bit of reason
Forget about the time
Finally got the rhyme
To keep the music alive.

Confused

Where have you been all this time?
Caught up in your personality
Too caught up to see the hate
Murder and police brutality
Lost and scared as the evil rises upon you
Shocked that we live with this
As if you didn't have a clue
Lost all your money, friends, and family
Alone on the streets suddenly not so manly
Find yourself putting a needle to your vein
As if the momentary relief will take away the pain
Lost and confused the evil is upon you
Still the same loving person at heart
Lord what did I do?

Prisoners

Millions gathered for the slaughter
Husband, wife, son and daughter
As they stood horrified
From the view of loving eyes
We rose against conformity
In the land and home of the free
They listened to the screams and cries
Crying as they watched their demise
Feel the presence of hell's beast
You're not welcome to the feast
As they stared horrified
Sight of death left them paralyzed
Nothing more, nothing to come
Prisoners of the beast in hell's kingdom
In the realm where murder is glorified
Laugh in the face death no longer horrified
Nothing more, nothing to come, no longer
Is there anything to run from?
As a tear dropped from its eye
Nothing but a memory of those who died

Escape With Me

How long will you wait for me?
The sun runs across the sky.
Will you come escape with me?
Let day turn into night

How long will you let me bleed?
The moon runs across the sky,
Tonight the savages feed.
There's an escape for you and I

Did you really wait for me?
Blood seeps from the sky,
Let it rain down on me,
No more suffering after you die!

Escape it all with me.
Gods, Angels fall from the sky.
You'll see the death of me,
Before we end tonight

Now you escaped with me
We'll dance across the sky
You'll run away with me
We live from high to high.......

My Love

The sun sets, what a beautiful sight
But if you where here I'd have much delight
Layin' in the grass, lettin' time float away
I'll tell you about my love today
Running through the clouds together
Drinkin' from the stream
You can stay with me forever
Please don't mind my friend Beam
Never said nothing I never knew
As I let time drift away
Let's do what we want to do
And live to see another day

Lab coat, rowdy goat
Frank Zappa might attack ya
Run you rabbit run!

Dove flew upside down
Robert was very peaceful
The TV melted

Obsession

I'm trying to beat you
I'm trying to meet you
I'm trying to let this pass by

I won't let them meet you
I won't let them beat you
I won't let the thought of you die

I've lost all interest
As God as my witness
You'll be in heaven tonight!

I'm dying to seek you
I'm trying to greet you
I'm watching as you pass me by

I won't help them meet you
I won't help them beat you
Why won't the thought of you die!

I'm lost I'm all sorrow, the sins of tomorrow
I woke up in hell tonight
I'm trying to greet you, I'm dying to meet you
I'm watching as you pass me....Bye

Scarlet Rose

Scarred tears fear of threat,
A scarlet rose of violet

Wrath of envy bred in fate,
Deadly scent of flowers illuminates
Bitter taste washes away the thoughts
Of the demon's evil plot

Scarred tears fear of threat,
A scarlet rose of violet

Endless hours consumed by time
Image of the damsel, who will soon be mine
Restful restlessness, what will I do,
With the insanity lurking in me and you?

Scarred tears fear of threat,
A scarlet rose of violet

We'll ride the waves of endless time
Lost in the possibilities of a wandering mind

Scarlet fear tears of threat,
A scarred rose of violence

Seeds of Life

The seeds of life enter my veins
The seeds of life take away the pain
These are my cries,
I'm trying to reach you please hear my cries
I'm dying without you.
No one spreads love so why must I?
No one cares who lives and dies,
Washed in demise, I'm dying
Without you, please hear the cries
I'm lost without you
The seeds of life enter the veins;
The seeds of life drove me insane.

Seeds of Life 2

The seeds of life enter my vein
Bring feelings of tranquility
Seeds of life take away my pain
Incense smoke swirls around my head
My mind running as I lay down for bed
The seeds of life enter my brain
They take over my body, take away the pain
The seeds of life make me closer to you
Let's fly together out on the vast sea
Without the seeds of life who would I be?

Stay True

Don't ever say I never tried
To spread my love to you
I looked you in the eye yet you still had to lie
Don't tell me I was never true
I had nothing but passion as I laid you
We used to talk every day
You would be by my side as I got blown away
Lay me down to sleep
As I mumbled gibberish
I would hold you as you weeped
I was open to you, yet you had another side
You sat and watched as I cried
Filled my head with nothing but lies
Now it is over between me and you
Oh baby I'm going to stay true
As I say I fuckin' hate you

Blue Sky

Wake up in the morning, I thank God I'm alive
Another beautiful day upon the outside
I told you I'd see you again, and this is no lie
Look up to the clouds in the bright blue sky

I've got DMB on the stereo
So I'm jammin' it looking at the grin on my face through
    the mirror
Looking unusually good I must admit
Girl I'm coming back soon, I would not lie
Looking up at the blue sky upon the outside

Let loose as we dance the mystical way
Grateful I found you on this bright sunny day
Don't want to be demanding but girl you've got to stay
Stay here with me while the sun rolls away

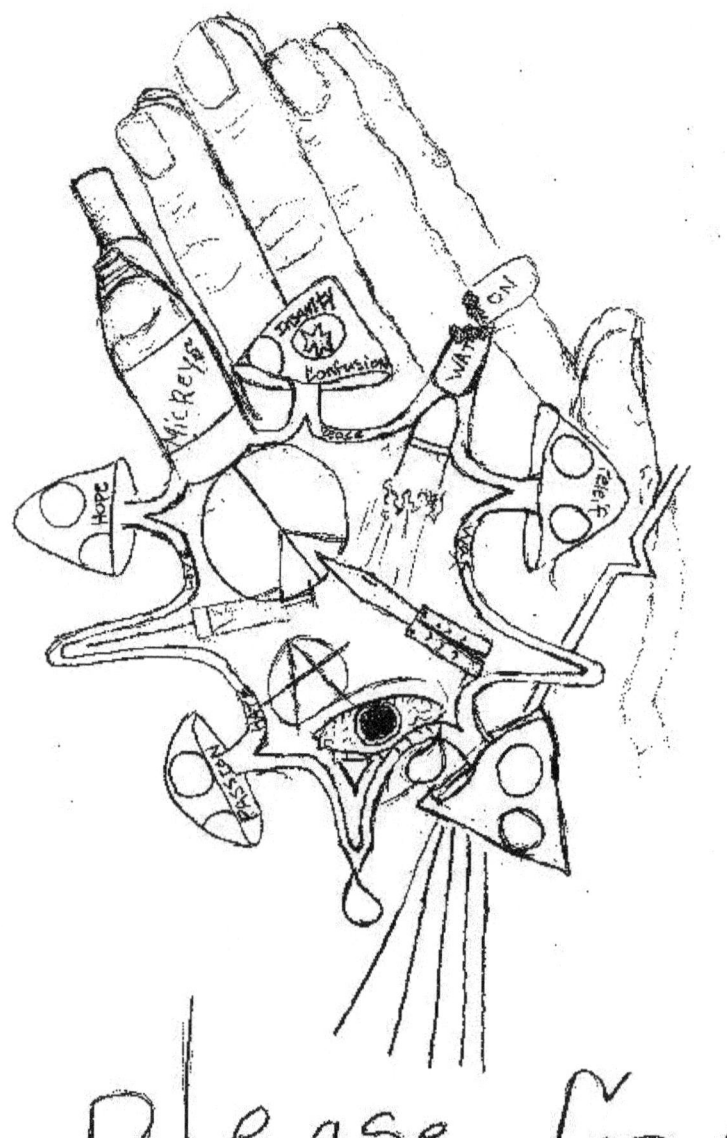

Government and Politics

Political IV

It's running through your veins,
It's running to your brain
The politics are here to stay

It's running from your veins
It eats at all the brains
Politics control day after day

It's a big issue, for those of you…
Who may be addicted.
You are now convicted

No need for a quick fix,
We've got some real kick,
Come take a hit off the Political IV

Jump on a board, only if you can afford
Such an act of senseless thinking
The political IV is here to stay

Illegal on the street,
In the white house, WHAT A TREAT!
Let's make it a pill and push it,

Clean up the streets,
We don't want to compete with the dirt on
    our feet
So let's start them up young, get them
    hooked,
They'll come, even a toddler loves the
    feeling

So numb…
                The Political IV OVERWHELMS US!

The Lynching

Once upon a bright sunny day, all the children ran off to play,
Adults all gathered into the town, you could smell the excitement,
The smiles were profound
They peered up at two men wearing hoods,
There were originally three, on escaped in the woods
These here are niggers the sheriff proclaimed
A despicable race that must be tamed
Nothing but disgrace to the white man's name
Like savages the crowd smelled the men's fear
Heartless human beings they were as they rave, ranted and cheered
They put the noose around each neck
Then took a step back on the big wooden deck
Any last words before you die?
Please take our hoods off so the crowd can look at our eyes
And they can cherish the moment they hear our last cries
As the deck dropped the bodies were quenching
Everyone had smiles, possessed by the lynching.

US Marines

Look at yourself, in the marines,
Joined the draft at the age of 18
They said it'd be fun
Bullets flying by got you on the run
Here's your chance to turn your life around
Bombs, gunshots, screaming the only sound
They said it'd be fun
Now there's a father without his son
His last breath was his last sound
Signed himself off to war, look what he found
They told you how to live and how to behave
They put your ass 6 feet beneath us sealed in a
    grave
You were just another marine
What you were told was a lie
Your family won't ever be seen from your eyes
You were sent to die, God Bless You US Marine

Aftermath

When there is love in the war
There will be nothing for the soldiers to fight for
No million dollar corruption to supply the
    ammunition
To them: what a ludicrous proposition
This is the way it is and the way it will be
Looking at myself through their eyes
There's no future for me
Little do they know I'll have the last laugh
As I travel the world and build from the aftermath

Corruption in the Government

Peer out the window at city streets
Corruption in the Government
As the riot police retreat
Cars blowing up in flames
The children went insane
On the ground, bodies with no names
People run the streets insane
No moon, no sun, nothing but fun
Nothing but the burn from acid rain
No police no laws
Corruption in the Government
Brought upon them from their flaws
Souls lost in regret
Tear gas fills the sky
Police no longer a threat
I am not afraid to die
No family no friends
Nothing but the end

Wizard cast a spell
Government controls us all
The mousey is fat

Anarchy Politics

We get misinterpreted from the government,
So they put on a news program and try to cover it.
Not with this generation, we're one of a kind.
Join together as one and we will find,
If we stand tall
They can't just kill us all.

Have we been forsaken?
Or just mistaken,
War will bring death and destruction,
But we already have that from political corruption
Just keep standing tall
And if they try to kill us all
Promise me you'll keep fighting until your last fall

Dooms Day
What about pollution?
There are nucs to test
Ain't no stoppin'
Until nothin's left

Flames burn up the sky
Mushroom cloud of death and destruction
Civilization of man left to die
A worldly slaughter
Everyone's allowed to join
Bring your own lethal weapon
Come to seek and destroy

What about the planet
There's plenty more
Fuck keeping the peace
When we can fight a war

Poison replaces oxygen
No one will survive
Last glimpse of the sky
Last day of feeling alive
There was never a future
Never a past

Never thought this could happen
Why'd we live so fast?
What about the world
That is no more

The fighting will stop
When there's nothing left to fight for

Forever Resistance

Resisting authority, there is such a thing
Throw a fist up as we come together and sing
My whole family has the black sock blues
If we fight together we will win, they will lose
Go through life forget the mans existence
We fight for the same cause
Forever resistance
Resisting government
Resisting conformity
Resist together against authority
Got my black socks and black shoes
We will fight together until they cry the blues
Come with us while the people rebel
We have a cause, they can go to hell
Let's stick together until the end of existence
Fight for the cause
Forever resistance

It's Time

I can sense the act of revulsion
People are rising who will lead this motion
The time is now the time is right
I can see clear, no one can see the light
Is this the end of the tunnel, or just the beginning?
Don't get these songs wrong it's the government
 I'm offending
This is a revolution, let's stop the war that's a
 solution
Will they listen? Fuck no!
So it's time for this president to fuckin' go
The time is now the time is right,
Mark these words we will put up a fight!

Government Abuse

I feel the presence, there's no remorse,
They're out to get you; an evil source.
We must be blind there's no excuse,
Just avoid the issue of government abuse.
You take the good and turn it to hell,
Go ahead, forget all the soldiers who fell
From the drugs we've used, we're lost and confused
Just been abused, by the government we refused
Religion or Drugs? Choose your escape
What about your future? Who says there's fate?
Riot police retreat, cares blow up in flames
Covering the ground lay bodies with no names
Souls lost in regret
Tear gas fills the sky, police no longer a threat
I am not afraid to die
We must be blind, no other excuse,
To avoid the issue of government abuse
What about the planet, there's plenty more
Why keep the peace
When we can fight a war?
A corrupted government ended it all
Divided we stand, alone we fall
Poison replaces oxygen,
No one will survive,
Last glimpse of the sky
Last day of feeling alive
There was never a future, never a past
Never thought this could happen
Life taken so fast
I'm not blind. I won't take an excuse
I'll fight the issue of government abuse
What about the world that is no more?

The fight will stop, when nothing remains to fight for.

U.S. ARMY

The American Dream?

BE ALL that you

Can BE...

Without the ARMY

Life

My Sun

In search for the people but,
I'm the only one
All the souls taken from the earth,
Now trapped in the sun

Millions have died, millions to come
Come and join me, as we burn in the sun

Look up to the heavens,
Missile planes fill the sky,
Run from the destruction they soon will try

Millions have died, millions to come
Come and burn me, as we run through the sun

The end of existence upon us too soon
All the sins of the world now trapped in the
      moon

Hell is upon us, it seeks its doom,
Death and destruction,
From the flower it blooms

No life to live, there's nothing to be,
After years of compassion my soul is taken
      from me
In paradise just as he said,
The moment of death is nothing to dread

Millions have cried, millions will come,
Come follow me as we live in the sun.

New Beginning

A new beginning or is this the end?
From the heavens the evil transcends

Anarchy is what I see
The screams and cries of his last pleas
Taste of murder in a world that kills
The bottomless hole the bodies soon fill

A new beginning or is this the end?
From the heavens the evil transcends

We love a world of chaos
A life once lived is now lost
Go ahead and try
Make it out alive
Through souls of sorrow try to survive

March to their death they hang their heads
Silent stench of flesh lingers from the dead

A new beginning or is this the end?
Sent from the heavens the devil has sinned
Sent from the heavens the devil has sinned

A new beginning for a heavenly end

New Beginning 2

Another day as the cool breeze blew by
As the dark clouds rolled across the sky
People looked to each other with fear and panic
Hell is upon us, it seeks its havoc
A new beginning or is this the end?
Helpless people turn to their best friend
A prophecy is what they all seek
The people to scared to rise up and speak
From the heavens the evil transcends
A new beginning or is this the end?
No smiles no love, they're filled with dread
March to their death as they hang their heads
A look at the aftermath made the strongest cry
That day it all ended, yet started it all
Death is inevitable; it too will soon call. . .

The Slaughter

Where are you?
Who am I?
We're somebody, somebody to die
There were screams
There were cries
There were tears in children's eyes
Everyone here was sent to die
Sent to die
I am you and you am I
When I leave no one will cry
Everyone sent to die
There was screaming
Human beings, being slaughtered
Everyone sent to die
There's a reason for me, a reason for you
With blood in your hands, what will you do?

The Pain

You don't know, the pain I feel inside
Though you know the pain of endless sky

I tried to save you
You stayed awake all night
Just for the pleasure
You drifted out of sight

Where'd it come from?
You don't even know
It's your misfortune
Trapped in its control

You know the sight of an endless sky
You don't know the pain I feel inside

Lost in the thought
Of endless time
You should know
To kiss me tonight

Live

We lost it all, with no delay,
Our weakness and insecurity, left on display
We've been thrown around, kicked and
    abused
Anything but love, keeps them amused
Where are we going, let's all go together
If your body don't make it, your soul lives
    forever
Live for today it may be your last
With a blink of an eye, your life went so fast
We've been sent away, kicked and abused
The sight of war keeps them amused
A glimpse of death left on display
The sight of the angel that took you away

Too Late

A sudden gun shot heard in the air
A family ruined, no one seemed to care
A glimpse of brutality, this is your future

Not knowing who you are, or if you care,
Reflection is nothing but a cold stare
Destructive thoughts lead to shattered dreams
Nothing at all... is what it seems

A family with no love
Whose prayers don't reach above
A sudden fear of the death that awaits
Most are scared, others anticipate
Leaving a world full of hate

Is this what it seems, did I already leave?
Nothing but a dream
Too late to turn back you're already there
Will someone help, did someone care?
Only yourself, is nothing but a stare

Night Death

Bolt the @#$@in' doors, no one here is safe
Darkness is amongst you, lost all your faith
You can run if you want, load your gun and try
One thing you won't forget! The night death filled the
    sky

We're coming to get you, collect the dead!
Violence and corruption, is what you're fed
We're coming to get you, bury the dead
I've already got you. I'm the one in your head

Christmas Feast

As I sit, and glance across the room
Aroma of roast and that loving jazz tune
Look at my mother, deep into her eyes
Try to tell her I love her but to paralyzed
Something to fill my expression besides blank
    meaningless eyes
So mysterious ... silent? Look the darkness creeps
    into the room
Have I left this world, my own reflection a mere
    costume?
I have died upon this Christmas day
A day to beautiful to take life away
Just one life to live so I lived it this way
To the fullest and to everyday
The reaper has taken my life away
Slipped into my loving house
Caught me with his sleek knife
I am the spirit of the confused son
I walk on the thin line of danger and fun

Didn't see my life pass and slip out of my hands
Didn't see the transaction from boy to man
Now I am company at my families Christmas feast
As peaceful as the ocean's tide, as scary as hell's
    beast

Feel blessed to have the loving family I do
One that will have a plate at the table
Always waiting for you

Girl

Get up every morning,
Just can't help thinking about you
The way you walk the way you talk
The way I get stuck in your eyes
Girl if you left me tomorrow
I don't know what I'd do
Besides cry and sing away the sorrow
That I feel, no love, no hate, no sex appeal

Lay down to go to bed and I'm thinking about

The day you leave me is the day I'll dread
Being with out you, lost and confused
With no one to talk to
If I could I'd be with you to the end
Girl what would I do, who would I be. . .
Without you?

Reflection

So you say you're true to yourself
Behind the lies, greed and wealth?
Take a look deep inside of you
A look deep inside of your mind
In this person will you stay true?
Look into your mind, what will you find
Staring at your own kind!
Personal reflection as you tilt your head to cry
Self reflection as you pray to God to die
Personal reflection is where you are today
Look up at your loved ones, beg them to stay...
Just another day
Looking at myself but from a different view
Looking up at the heavens God what should I
      do?!
Self reflection made a tear come upon my eye
My last reflection, is today your day to die...
Death comes at any given moment
Yourself. Your life, how will you own it. . .?

Brutality

Is today the last day of human existence?
Nothing but sinners running our lives
Rise to the murder, our only resistance
Looking at the world through blood shot eyes
Manson and Bush are one in the same
Murders in the street, who's to blame?
Caught up in other affairs
Another soldier sent away and dies
Yet the president doesn't seem to mind
Look into the world with blood shot eyes
Murders sentence to execution
Is this violence's only solution?
Stop brutality with brutality
Another murderer running our country, this is reality
Murder is murder, a life, you took it
Cover it all up with innocent lies
Save us the money and tears, please commit suicide

Couldn't handle the world... without blood shot eyes

The Plot

A young girl to weak, to stand up and speak
Rose to another day with much dismay
Put a smile on her face, to cover up her depressive state
Then shit gets complicated, or so it seems
She looks to the guy, she never dated
As the girl plots and schemes
Never had much faith for up above
Always was rejected when she reached out for love
Acts and looks as if nothing is wrong
For in her head she recites such a mournful song
Did she see the unusual bright light
When the girl hung herself in the attic last night?

My Last Kiss

Finally I'm free from evil and hate,
Free from the horror we contemplate
Where is my destiny?
The evil is after me
Finally caught up to me in the abyss,
Then took my life with its deadly kiss
This is my last kiss, this is my last kiss

Where are we going? Let's all go together,
If your body won't make it your soul will live
    forever,
Live for today it may be your last,
In the blink of an eye your life has passed
This is my last kiss, shadows of seeking eternal
    bliss
This is my last kiss

You set me free from evil and hate,
Free from the horror I contemplate
There is no destiny, the evil have captured me
Look in my eyes, listen to this
My last kiss
This is my last kiss, glimpse of death
Left on display, the sight of the Angel who
    takes you away
This is my last kiss

My Last Kiss 2

Running through the dark (abyss)
Not knowing my destiny
I can't take much of this
The evil is out to get me
I can sense it on my tracks
Running from this unknown source
Its love is vengeance, it seeks my remorse
It caught me inside the (abyss)
It takes my life with one deadly kiss
His love is vengeance, his hate compassion
Not even the strong have the courage to catch him
He'll catch us all, don't try to run
For this is his game, this is his fun
Look at me and listen to this
It's the last time you see me
It's my last kiss

Blue tree distorted
The sunset was riveting
Yellow submarine

Lost Soul

I am a loving hateful freak
Finding true love in such a hateful world is what I seek
On a journey to find a lost soul
Seems impossible, trapped in the dark hole
It causes me much fright
To know that the people won't unite
Too ignorant to hear me when I speak
Vengeance in such a loving world is what I now seek
No one spreads love so why must I?
No one cares whether or not we live or die
Seems almost impossible in this dark hole
Almost impossible to find my lost soul

Lost Control

Running across a haze of insane people
Rummaging through the streets with no home
Hopeful youths with no direction
Feelings are lost, no place to go

You've lost all control!
Caught up across the globe
No citizens to patrol
A wasteland of our worst dreams

Hopeless youths with no direction
Where to live amongst the creeps
Sex and drugs, our only protection
For such a harsh reality

You've got no control
Chaos across the globe
 Put us in the hole
Take a look at the anarchy
Take a look at reality

Running in a daze of mixed emotion
Not sure whether to stay or go
A costly price for a bad intention
You've lost all control

Limits

Testing the limits,
Putting myself to the test
Internal behavior
Trying to be the best

Trying to let go, let go of the fear inside
Running forever because tomorrow
It's live or die

Mental confusion
But I've been here before
Dying inside
Building off the internal core

No one around me
But there's someone to live for
Trying to drowned me
To see what I have in store

Testing the limits
Putting myself to the test
Is there regrets?
When there is nothing left?

Inside My Head

Trapped inside my head
Am I confused?
I didn't mean to leave you
Yet I was too amused

The mind will attack
Run if you can
You won't escape it
A prodigy of man

Trapped inside my head
My only refuge
Don't be so scared,
Of what a mind can construe

I didn't mean to hurt you
With the power of your brain
Where everyone's insane
Too amusing
To put down the remote
Washed up in the nonsense
Intentionally provoked

Trapped inside my head, I
Don't mind the stay, my
Mind is my refuge; a sanctuary
For the imagination to play

Freedom

Life is good, we are strong
Let the people unite as one
Let's defeat them
Let's fight for freedom
What is it for?
We send our children off to war
Let's rise to freedom
Stand strong to beat them
We don't need violence to bring peace
Why should we hide this from police?
Where is our freedom?
Why did they have to beat him?
Let's just have fun
We can reach this unite as one
We can beat them
In the fight for freedom

The magical being speaks the truth giving me
forever lasting faith in God

feelings

This alcohol is poison inflicting much pain
It is my enemy and also my friend, killing my soul
Intoxicating my brain, healing my anger
Leaving me numb to my senses such as cocaine
Can it really come to this?
Why not speak the truth?
We are all addicted to drugs
Whether it's from the streets, the liquor store or the
 doctor's office
Whether you support it or deny
Live it or try it
This label is poison inflicting much pain
Politician, democrat, or republican
Jock, stoner, genius, and geek
How about a human nothing more nothing less
A human, not a title
Label, word, or race
Just a human being
With feelings, of love, hate
And fear, feelings of passion,
And desire, feelings of insanity
When left in despair
This feeling is poison inflicting much pain
These feelings are natural yet I'm left insane

Darkness

Nothing but havoc, is all I see
Nothing but darkness following me
There's no emotion in a world of hell
Did I lose my mind? Too tough to tell

Darkness amongst you lost all your faith
A sight you won't forget, the night death filled the
    sky
I'm just a spirit just like the rest trapped in the
    darkness
I must confess

They're coming for you, bury the dead
I've already trapped you
I'm the one in your head

Darkness surrounds me, what should I do?
With blood seeping hands, what would you do?
I'm just a spirit just like the rest
Trapped in the darkness I must confess

Crazy aren't We All

Crazy aren't we all?
Looking at the relentless wall
You did call me crazy just the other day
You would be too if you had the guts to stay
Stay with me as I lose my mind
      You'll lose everything
       But your soul you will find
Travel to the center of a complex brain
We'll go together, we'll both go insane
We are all a little crazy I'm sure
Don't go to the doctor, there is no cure
You might be confused, even scared
I warned you to come if you dared
Things got distorted as I disappeared in
      THE WALL
A little bit crazy aren't we all?

All the Souls Taken

In search for the people but I'm the only one
All the souls taken from the earth, now trapped in
    the sun
Look up to the heavens, missile planes fill the sky
Run away from the destruction they will soon try
The end of existence has come upon us too soon
All the sins in the world now trapped in the moon
No life to live, there's nothing to be
After years of compassion my soul is taken from
    me
I'm in paradise, just as he said
The day of death, is nothing to dread

Voices in my Head

I hear voices in my head,
Singing to me
Lay down for bed
Voices, voices in my head
Contradicting what I said
Why are there voices in my head?

I have gone all out insane
I find it hard, to maintain
I hear voices in my head
Contradicting what you said
Voices, voices in my head
When they stop I must be dead
Fuck these voices in my head

Turn On the Lights

This is the last poem I will try to write
You see its late, time to say good night!
A long list of nothing for my dismay
Must get some rest for such a long day...
Before I leave I thought I might ask
Is that your face or is it a mask
Sshh! That noise be quiet, you hear?
Such a tough task to look at your ear
Turn on the lights and run off to bed
Can't get any sleep with these ants in my head
Or in my pants! Would you care to dance?
Like a zombie in a trance?
But if it stops and comes to an end
End you say? Did I say this too?
For I never said anything that I never knew
If it's the end do you have a bed?
You could lend for such a good friend
What a splendid slumber inside my head
Turn on the lights and run off to bed

Troubled Dreams

Please put a rest
To these troubled screams
Delusional victims
Lost in a dream

So I drift away, inside my head
To find a broken vision
Of unraveling dread

Please put a rest
To my troubled dreams
These haunted victims
Love brutality

Walk through the fog
Just a mortal, am I...
I put myself to the test
Dignity to justify
I put it all out to rest
Another victim am I?
Don't wait for nothing left
Just a soul when you die

Tonight

I'm trying to beat you,
I'm trying to meet you
I'm trying to let this pass by

I won't let them meet you
I won't let them beat you
I won't let the thought of you die

I've lost all my interest
As God as my witness
You'll be in heaven tonight

I'm trying to beat you
I'm dying to meet you
I'm watching as you pass me by

I won't help them meet you
I will help them beat you
Why won't the thought of you die?

I'm lost in my sorrow
The sins of tomorrow
I woke up in hell tonight

These are my cries,
I'm trying to reach you,
please hear my cries,
I'm dying without you,
washed in their demise,
I'm lost without you please here the cries

The Silence has Stricken Me

No words for expression
The silence has stricken me
No use for communication
As you look at me, helpless without protection
The silence has stricken me
The silence spreads like infection
Here I am lost and confused
The mental escape keeps me amused
Can't face you with a tear in my eye
Not happy or sad so why must I cry?
The silence has stricken me, but why
Tried to express myself but I just stared
Want to tell you I love you and how much I
    cared
The silence has stricken me, made me cry
The silence has stricken me as I lay down with
    fright
Silence is upon me as I died in your arms tonight

Serpents Requiem

This is a maddened requiem, singing
From the serpents tongue
To the gullible he deceives
The hate in your blood is swelling
He will reign if you believe
Insane cries, not worth yelling
Brutality upon those who try

You will sing the glorious requiem
Psychotic is the serpent's tongue
Ambitious torture oppresses the free
For those who conspire the wrath of the fire

Will viciously be stung, from the poison
In the serpent's tongue
Sound from the insane requiem, singing
From the serpent's tongue,
His dark shadow creeps over you
Trapped in hell's realm what will I do!
You try a sudden anarchist revolt
Trying to overcome him with a malicious
      assault
But you don't realize the immorality
Singing the serpent's requiem is your reality

Far Away

Today I feel the need to travel to a far off land
To escape from these rules and regulations
So I took what was in my hand
Something to help it go down was in great demand
But I'll feel the same either way
So I figure it'll be ok
Is it already another day?
A last it came on ever so pleasingly fast
Is that a problem, oh no!
But I sure did step outside to hear the wind blow
Sun was out, or is that the moon?
As Zappa put it.... I'm a dental floss tycoon
My friends thought I might be fakin',
I must have been mistaken
I thought the whole world was shakin'
It was obvious to my company that I was bakin'
Have I eaten my hand or just what was in it?
Who am I talking to, did I offend it?
Today was different I seemed to believe it
These crazy thoughts, my mind conceived it
I suddenly realized there was nobody, nothing at all
After all this, these peoples' opinions and worries
    seemed so small
As I walked to the gas station I realized everyone
    could use some self exploration

Silent Souls

The silent souls fly through the sky
  No time for sorrow
No time to cry

Chorus   You will not be the one to take
My life from me
  Many try and many fail,
  I'll meet with them in hell

Silent souls flying all around
My life is gone look what I have found
The remorse of the dead
Why are there voices in my head?

I can't take it no more
The flying spirit of the whore

Why do we live this way?
  In a world full of nothing
There's nothing today

There is now nothing
Nothing at all
Divided we stand
Alone we all fall

On the Edge

A scent in the air so mischievous
The smile on your face, a look so devious
I'm on the edge today, killing myself
Another life that went astray
Mamma, please look the other way
Your little boy's on the edge, took his life today
Never been good enough with anything I do
If I stay longer, I don't know how I'll make it through
Keep your distance I'm on the edge today
Caught up in the world, so I took myself away
Finally I'm free from the evil and hate
Finally I'm free from the horror I contemplate
People may think I didn't take this serious
The smile on my face
Made the story so mysterious

Day of Death

    In search for the people, but I am the only one.
    All the souls taken from the earth,
    Now trapped in the sun,
Chorus
    Look up to the heavens, missile planes fill the sky,
    Run away from the destruction, they will soon try.
    The end of existence upon us too soon,
    All the sins in the world now trapped in the moon.
Chorus
    No life to live, there's nothing to be,
    After years of compassion my soul is taken from me.
    I'm in paradise, just as he said,
    The day pf death is nothing to dread.

Chorus Day of Death nothing to fear,
    The day of death is finally here!

Idioms Explained

Common Idioms

Have you ever heard any idioms? Sure you have! Idioms are used all over the world. They are groups of words that have no real meaning when broken down, but when the words are put together there is always a lesson to be learned.

Hundreds of idioms exist and most are still used today, but where did all these idioms come from? Well, there is not a single derivation that produced all idioms; they originated from many sources. Some from the Bible, Navajo tradition, horse racing, and others are from famous storytellers such as Shakespeare or Homer; who would often use them to spice up their writings (Terban).

Most idioms teach a lesson about propriety. One common idiom is "to have a chip on one's shoulder". When reading particular idioms without knowing the meaning it becomes very confusing. This peculiar idiom originated in nineteenth-century America from a boy who thought he was "pretty tough". The boy would put a wood chip on his shoulder and dare anyone to knock it off. Today the idiom refers to anyone who is "touchy", or takes offense easily (Terban). Sometimes people who have a chip on their shoulder are snobbish, or stuck up. No matter the situation anytime there is an idiom used toward someone I suggest looking up the meaning, who knows to what they are referring!

"I cannot wait until I can strip this overbearing medieval costume off of my sweaty figure". "I mean jeez you'd think that they'd give as a break, at least a half-hour break!" "What do you think Rofus?" "Why uh I happened to like the tire swing." "I knew it, Rofus you're a complete moron, but I love you, I have to… because on this dreaded day, this horrible, tedious, scrutinizing day you happen to be dressed as my lady!"

Any normal person would turn down the bribe to pretend you're in love with a two hundred pound eight graded, with half a brain, and no need to wear a padded bra. I have to act, all day, as if I need to sell pigs for my lady (Rofus) in order to gain her love.

Medieval freaks come out of the woodwork to rummage around and imagine the medieval times in our make shift market like stage. These people buy live animals and what not, just as one would in the medieval days. Then head back to their houses in the boonies and like the pioneer lifestyle they love.

Thanks to the drama club, my mom made me sign up for; I have to take part in fair like this, which our town comes up with spontaneously every month. This time though I had I trick up my sleeve.

The previous night I had done some research on medieval fairs, the research I was researching happened to mention that a common idiom had developed from the pig selling booths. They would trick the customers into buying a pig concealed in a bag, and tell the customer not to open it until they had gone far away. When the customer opened the bag, a cat would come out, symbolizing the saying that stands today for revealing a secret to a con trick. (Stevenson)

This is exactly what I've been doing all morning. I am allergic to cats, I hate them, when my sister came home with a dozen more cats from the shelter I was a sniveling mess. I realized what had to be done, so I did it! I've been selling my sisters cats, conning medieval groupies, and avoiding Rofus' charm.

Well the next thing I know the director for the drama club reports to our booth/stage. This could only mean trouble, there in his hands were two of those damned cats that I hate. I was playing it cool, telling him how Rofus let a hobo was sleep in the pig stall, and how the hobo had fifteen cats on leashes and what not. He was buying it he really was, then Rofus had to let it slip, he let the cat out of the bag and revealed my devious con trick.

That was strike three and here in California that's life in prison! I repeat life in prison! For selling pigs man, like that's some serious business, well any ways the moral is don't sell crank to your auntie, work the corner as JoJo the clown, and definitely do not sell cat for pigs, the court system doesn't take this lightly!

That Crow Saying

"As the crow flies, fifty-seven more kilometers, as the crow flies," replied the midget of a man in the tan tour guide outfit.

"As the crow flies," I thought to myself, "what is with the odd little man sitting next to me? He's been blurting weird sayings with no apparent meaning all day. He refers to these as some sort of idiom language."

"Then we will be in slug heaven, keep in mind that this is quite illegal. I could lose my job if this information got out."

"Zuke, please spare me with all that paranoia jazz, it's an in and out operation, all I need is a little time to collect the slime from about 1,457 slugs, but please tell me where did you get that crow saying, little fella?"

"Oh, I'm glad you asked, it is an old eighteenth century term that refers to the shortest distance from one place to another," said the minute companion. "Ok, now it's coming into view, might I ask one last thing?"

"Why certainly!"

"Could you possibly get that gerbil out of my lunch box," I shrieked in pure horror!

"Why You Cryin?"

It was a cool Fall afternoon down in the bayou, and Lyle (the biggest croc that swims these murky waters) was indeed crying. In fact this monstrous crocodile, believe it or not, cries every day, except for every other Sunday, that shines a full moon, but that's irrelevant.

"Oh shoot!" Lyle thought to himself, "here comes Slater the gaiter, if he sees me crying this will surely spread all over the swamp, and if it does the vicious alligator gang, nicknamed the "Crocodile Killa's" will surely be after me and my pad. Alright Lyle calm down, focus on something fun, something pleasant, go to your happy place." It was too late for any of this nonsense, a gigantic croc like this doesn't have a happy place, he's a predator for Pete sake, one of the meanest on the block.

Slater came slithering up through the muck, " What's happening Lyle my man? You up for checking the babes at Newton's Tavern?"

Lyle avoided eye contact, " Oh that crazy newt finally got that joint running huh, well gee, I'm sorry brotha, but uh, I, uh have some stuff to do around here at the pad, some uh paintings to finish and what not."

"What the? Some paintings huh," say Lyle.

Slater let out a chuckle "why are you cryin?"

" Crying" Lyle let out, as if he was about to let some serious tears fly, " I am not crying to show weakness, all crocodiles cry." "Nice Lyle," he thought to himself, "stay on you toes buddy." If the truth were known, Lyle wasn't sure why crocodiles cry or whether or not it was just he.

Just then an overwhelming net swept the both of them into its web like structure. Slater cried out the most feminine snarl a gaiter could produce. Next they heard, "Ah Wow! What we got here is very rare, a gaiter and croc that appear to be mingling with each other, or maybe they just caught the fancy of one another."

Lyle was horrified, not only did Slater see him crying but also now the whole world may see it as well, he prayed to God this Joe didn't have good ratings. Which he doubted he did, based on that tacky safari tour guide outfit.

" Aye Jimbo, why don't ya come outta the raft there and get a close up of this crocodile's beautiful fangs compared to that of the putrid alligator?"

"Oh no, Jeff, ah, I'll leave that to you, I can get a decent shot from where I'm at, plus uh, I have an ingrown toe nail…"

" Well that's fine then mate, but take a look at this fella with the zoom button. As you can see here, we caught this croc crying."

Lyle tried to struggle free but this guy was some sort of croc master, and apparently knew how to hold these beasts from biting his face or even a phalange. Either that or he was just flat out crazy, and had good luck for escaping scenarios like this. Lyle stopped struggling when he heard the croc man say, " Aye it's alright little fella all crocodiles cry."

"Did he just call me little fella? This guy is going to get it." By now Slater had given up and was trying to work up some tears himself.

"You see," the croc man said, " it was once thought that crocodiles' unique glands in their upper jaw release tears which flow to their mouths to help moisten their food. Every now and then you'll see one basking in the sun with their jaws propped open just right to release these tears. They do not cry over emotion so these are fake tears. But take a look at this gaiter, what he is trying to produce is crocodile tears, or " fake tears." " Why does he do this?" "Uh, it even fools me, he must be really scared or desperate to try to pull the old crocodile tears trick, but hey, it worked for O.J. Simpson didn't it?" "Alright fellas I'm gonna let ya go now, be nice and don't bite old Jeff, aye?"

The two reptiles lay stunned as Jeff let them go and jumped back in his motorized raft. " Aye look at that water python over there, Jimbo, lets get moving."

After the two watched Jeff and his plump cameraman slowly make their way across the swamp. Slater let out a little sniffle, Lyle looked at him, "hey man, why you cryin?"

"Forget about it Slater, I won't tell anyone you cry like a girl, lets head over to Newton's huh? If we leave now we may even make "Happy Hour."

They swam towards Newton's just as the sun was setting and illuminating a neon pink/orange array that loomed in the fog that was now beginning to cover the swamp for the evening. No one ever found out about the story and all the crying that took place on that day, and you can bet you bottom dollar Slater didn't have any luck with the ladies that evening, furthermore that they both lived happily ever after.

Fight Fire With Fire

Here I am, running through the crowd like a wild maniac. Although, I do fit in, I can spot at least a dozen more people participating in this giant heavy metal circle dance. I can't help it, something has come over me, I've become possessed, locked in a mental revolution of musical mayhem.

The culprit, Metallica Live, blasting "Fight Fire with Fire" from their amplified stereo speakers, at a sound decimal that can paralyze the weak.

Well I made it down front; I wonder where my friends ran off too? I look back at the pure chaos I ventured from, absolute madness. Seven bonfires now lit up in general admission in tribute to the song I'm sure.

Suddenly I have a flash back, to when my grandpa told me, in his forest ranger days they had to fight fire with fire in order to stop forest fires. Burn out the path the fire is destined to blaze. How could this be? (Cambridge University Press)

Now I was bursting in fear, this overwhelmed my body to the point where I felt nauseated; those Chili Cheese Fritoes did a number on me in the humidity.

Now I face a contained, controlled, designated area of madness for buffoons who can't control themselves with music this loud.

"Wow the pit has nearly tripled in a matter, of seconds," I thought as I mustered up every last bit of strength I had, the ending is near.

"I'm going to have to fight fire with fire," was the last thing heard as I ran into the heavy metal abyss that few dare to chance.

Quite the Voyage

"Wow! Maybe I shouldn't be doing this… maybe I'm not the man for the job. This is dangerous! We could get seriously hurt! Someone could die! Man o' man I'm shuttin' her down, I have to, don't I?"

The cabin door suddenly swung open, there stood Herald, the ugliest man on "Sweet Mother Earth". He's cross-eyed, reasonably chubby, his face is mashed in (sort of like a Pug, which is a very ugly dog) plus, on top of that, he smelled like sauerkraut and jelly beans.

"Hey there, Skip, jeez you sure are driving swell! Keep it up."

"Is that so, Herald? Am I really pullin' this off? I knew I could handle the captain's spot while he rests from the stomach bug."

"Move it, Herald! Get out of my way you Hobbit."

"I glanced over to the cabin entrance, it was Jeffery my main man from high school, he was trying to get past Herald, but that man moves like a slug."

"Skip, what in Sam's Hell are yea doin'? Kill the engine we're headin' for a ice burg!" screamed Jeffery.

"Alright, alright, the engine is killed mate but we are still moving too fast, we need to abandon ship."

" Are yea kiddin' me Skip? Did you forget we are in the Antarctica and that this cargo ship has been maxing out at about twenty five ever sense you ripped the prop off the other engine?" replied Jeffery. He looked very agitated; he's been on the edge ever sense I drank his stinkin' badger's milk, how should I know it was his last carton?

Suddenly the midget we picked up at our last stop (I decided to name him Thatious, he couldn't tell us his name, he only speaks sign language and nobody aboard went to college so the little man is out of luck) ran into the room. He tugged on my daisy doots, squealed in his favorite high pitch squeal and started doing something funny with his hands I suppose it's that sign language nonsense again.

"Hey Skip," Jeffery said, "I think that Thatious is trying to tell us something."

"Yes, Jeffery, I know, but what?"

By now it was too late, maybe it was that darn wasabi we bought from the Eskimos, or the mountain smoke we picked up from the conquistadors, I'm not sure what it was, but something knocked our senses off that cold December night. We did hit the rock, with full force; which wasn't much due to my faux pas the previous night.

"Herald go check for any damage to the stern… uh sternum, the front of the boat! Thatious, my miniature companion, go tell the captain that we decided to beach her for a little while, let that engine cool down." Thatious looked back at me with a blank stare, then nodded his head and departed from the cabin.

Jeffery was on the radio calling for help, no response.

"Well you really did it this time Skip," said Jeffery. He turned and left the cabin.

For a brief moment I almost broke down and cried, then I remembered the time I accidentally blew up Jeffery's new car, I let out a giggle, man was he pissed off! That could have been worse than our current scenario.

Two weeks later we were standing on the deck, the water had frozen around us and I couldn't possibly see how this little boat approaching was going to possibly help us out of this one. As the boat got closer I noticed the power it possessed as it broke through thick layers of ice.

"Hopefully these lads will help us, huh Skip?" said Jeffery. "Whatever you do, don't let Harold break the ice. He might scare them away, huh?"

"Aye lads, over there huh, hey would you mind helping us out over here, aye?"

"Sure, sure it's our job mate, we explore these waters for ships that have broken down and frozen in place, I know our boat may not look to appealing but this baby cruises though the thick ice like a warm knife through butter."

We were on our way in no time, we had that little tugboat clear a path, and we traded them Thatious in return. The captain is back and to my dismay I have to mop the poop deck, it's a crummy job but it has to be done, this is where I come into play

Redemption

Looking up towards the sky,
Will my savior rescue me or shall I lay here to die?
Is this the end, or just the beginning?
If my soul makes it to heaven I'll still be winning
As I lay to rest
Take off the bullet proof vest
God is my only protection
Keep me from sins that seem to be a spreading infection
Let out the hit with sterile eyes
Can't seem to move my body as I lie paralyzed
Looking up towards the sky
Put my head down as I start to cry
Based on self reflection
I tend to ask myself the question
Why? Why must we all die? Will I make it to a better place?
Or will I leave this realm from a gun shot to the face?
Just like some have been known to do
As I put the blunt down and tell myself I'm through
Never said I'm scared of death
But when it comes will I be blessed?
At my funeral I'll be looking my best,
Properly dressed
When it came to redemption I didn't think twice
Now I'm with my savior, in paradise......

www.ingramcontent.com/pod-product-compliance
Lightning Source LLC
Chambersburg PA
CBHW032058150426
43194CB00006B/572